Merry Christmas Daniel

Love,
    Grandpa & Grandma Gitchel

To Our Parents

TEACH ME ABOUT THE HOLY SPIRIT
© 1990 by Linda Sattgast & Jan Elkins
Published by Multnomah Press
Portland, Oregon 97266

Printed in Hong Kong

Library of Congress Cataloging-in-Publication Data

Sattgast, L. J., 1953-
    Teach me about the Holy Spirit / by L.J. Sattgast and Jan Elkins ; illustrated by Russ Flint.
      p. cm.
    Summary: Unlike her sister Flossie, who insists on having her own way, Flora obeys God and receives love, joy, self-control, and other gifts from the Holy Spirit.
    ISBN 0-88070-384-9
    1. Holy Spirit—Juvenile literature. [1. Holy Spirit. 2. Christian life] I. Elkins, Jan.
II. Flint, Russ, ill. III. Title.
BT121.2.S27   1990
234'.13—dc20

                                                90-35422
                                                CIP
                                                    AC

90 91 92 93 94 95 96 97 98 99 - 9 8 7 6 5 4 3 2 1

Teach me about
THE HOLY SPIRIT

By L.J. Sattgast & Jan Elkins
Illustrations by Russ Flint

MULTNOMAH
Portland, Oregon 97266

Flora and Flossie are twins.
They may look alike, but they
don't act alike.

Flora wants to obey God.
She asks the Holy Spirit to help her
do what is right. But Flossie wants
to have her own way.

When Aunt Mabel comes to visit,
Flossie doesn't even say hello.

The Holy Spirit gives Flora LOVE.
She hugs and kisses Aunt Mabel.
"I'm glad to see you!" she says.

Flossie sees a toy and wants it.
She fusses and pouts when she
can't have it.

The Holy Spirit gives Flora JOY.
She is happy with what she has.

Flossie is afraid when she visits
the doctor. She begins to cry
and carry on.

The Holy Spirit gives Flora
PEACE. She knows the doctor is
only trying to help her.

"Me first!" yells Flossie, running
for the slide.

The Holy Spirit gives Flora
PATIENCE. She waits in line
for her turn.

Flossie snatches a toy away from
cousin Jeremy.
"That's mine!" she says.

The Holy Spirit gives Flora
KINDNESS. "Here, Jeremy. You
can play with my balloons."

After eating, Flossie quickly leaves
the table and begins to play.

The Holy Spirit gives Flora
GOODNESS. She helps carry the
dirty dishes to the sink.

Flossie throws her books on the
floor when she is done with them.

The Holy Spirit gives Flora
FAITHFULNESS. She takes good
care of her books.

Flossie is mean to the kitty and
chases him away.

The Holy Spirit gives Flora
GENTLENESS. She pets the kitty
softly and listens to him purr.

"Don't touch the cake!" says Flossie's mother. But Flossie sneaks a lick of icing anyway.

The Holy Spirit gives Flora SELF-CONTROL. She waits until after dinner for dessert.

Flossie is miserable most of the
time. "The Holy Spirit can help you
obey God," says Flora. Flossie prays,
"Holy Spirit, please help me obey God."

Just then Dad calls.

"Who will bring me some wood?"

"We will!" say Flora and Flossie.

But the fruit of the Spirit is love, joy, peace, patience, kindness, goodness, faithfulness, gentleness and self-control (Galatians 5:22,23).

Helpful hints for parents about the
HOLY SPIRIT

PREPARATION FOR THE FRUIT OF THE SPIRIT
- Pray for your child. Ask God to give him a responsive heart that isn't resistant to you or to the Lord.
- Teach your child about God by reading the Bible, attending church, etc.
- Ask God to show you his heart and priorities often. Invite him to change any "barren or unfruitful" areas in your life.

DEFINITIONS OF FRUIT
LOVE: Showing people that you care about them. Being nice to other people whether you like them or not.
JOY: Being happy, even when you can't have your way or do what you want.
PEACE: Being quiet, not fussing, not being afraid.
PATIENCE: Being able to wait for something, not complaining.
KINDNESS: Helping others, being friendly.
GOODNESS: Obeying, doing nice things for others.
FAITHFULNESS: Taking care of your things, doing what you know is right, keeping your promises.
GENTLENESS: Being nice, soft, or careful with people, animals, toys, etc.
SELF-CONTROL: Doing what God wants. Not doing what you want to do when you know it's wrong.

TEACHING THE FRUIT OF THE SPIRIT
- As you read this book to your child, help her think of other ways to demonstrate each fruit.
- Teach your child to depend on Jesus to produce the fruit of the Spirit in his life, rather than trying to change himself by his own efforts.
- Explain to your child how her life affects other people—her actions can either help them or hurt them.
- Deal with disobedience, or the fruit of the Spirit cannot grow. Consider it an opportunity to train your child.
  —Don't yell instructions across the room. Get close to your child, lower your voice, and talk eye to eye.
  —Explain the consequence of disobedience. This will help your child accept responsibility for his actions.

—Follow through with firm but loving discipline if necessary.
- Praise and reward good behavior, especially acts of kindness initiated on her own.
- Teach your child to keep on trying when he fails miserably, because God is faithful, and he will help him.

CAUTION
- Look for reasons and motives behind misbehavior—is your child hungry, tired, sick, being mistreated by his friend, etc.? Perhaps a change of pace or a creative project can calm the turbulence.
- Look at the motives behind your actions—is there anger, harshness, or a need to control or criticize?
- Guard against things that would undermine your child's love and confidence in God, such as the type and amount of TV watched, the influence of friends, etc.
- Don't overreact. Giving more attention to wrong behavior can actually encourage it.
- Your child will often grow and produce fruit through making mistakes, so have patience and watch God work.

ADDITIONAL SUGGESTIONS
- Help your child find ways to be kind and thoughtful to other people. Teach him to be sensitive to those who are different from him—other races, the handicapped, etc.
- Teach your child to be kind to animals and nature.
- Don't discourage your child when she wants to give away a toy.
- When your child exhibits a fruit of the Spirit, praise it by name, e.g. "I like the way you put away your toys. You were being faithful!"
- When your child doesn't exhibit the fruit of the Spirit, seize the opportunity to teach, e.g. "What would have been the kind thing to do?"
- Since love is the fulfillment of the fruit of the Spirit, show your child God's love by how you love her. Hug, hold, praise, and speak the words, "I love you." Let her know that you have delight in her!